LIFE ON THE TRADING DESK

Hilarious Tales from a Group of Traders

Henrique M. Simões

Copyright © 2024 Henrique M. Simões

All rights reserved

The characters and events portrayed in this book are fictitious. Any similarity to real persons, living or dead, is coincidental and not intended by the author.

No part of this book may be reproduced, or stored in a retrieval system, or transmitted in any form or by any means, electronic, mechanical, photocopying, recording, or otherwise, without express written permission of the publisher.

To the traders who face the market's ups and downs with humor and grit. May these stories bring you a smile and a moment of joy.

TABLE OF CONTENTS

Preface

Revealing the Characters: Meet the Traders

Trading with the Gods

The IPO

Morning Midas

The Impossible Streak

Double Trouble

The Queen of Quant

The Signal that Misled Carter

A Seismic Trade

The Water Bottle Mystery

Slim Profits

From Dates to Deals

The Bagel Shop Trade

A Misunderstanding of Feline Proportions

Juicy Trade

Surfing the Markets

The Three-Word Challenge

Split Saga

Pig Panic

Copper Glow

From Vegas to Wall Street: The Victor Fortune Story

LIFE ON THE TRADING DESK

Preface

This book is a collection of humorous short stories set in a prop trading firm, where traders gather to navigate the stock market. Rivalries, conflicts, and envy drive the characters through vivid and entertaining episodes.

Inspired by real individuals I've encountered during my career in trading—across brokerage firms and hedge funds—these stories reveal the colorful personalities that fill the trading world.

The brokerage is a melting pot of diverse characters, from seasoned veterans to eager newcomers, each with their own unique approach to the market. Amid the hum of trading terminals and the clamor of ringing phones, tensions build as rivalries simmer, conflicts flare, and envy sparks, propelling the narrative with energy and intensity.

Whether it's the fierce competition for high-stakes deals or the camaraderie forged through shared victories and defeats, these tales offer an engaging glimpse into the human drama behind the financial markets. So sit back, relax, and enjoy the journey into the world of trading.

REVEALING THE CHARACTERS: MEET THE TRADERS

John Spinner is a reckless trader and compulsive gambler, is driven by impulse and finds himself constantly at the mercy of his trades. He epitomizes the emotional and impulsive trader, often falling prey to enthusiasms that result in significant losses. With the finesse of a bull in a China shop, John charges through the market without restraint. Coupled with his rough appearance, uncouth manners, and unrefined language, he navigates the market with all the grace of a junkyard dog.

Vivian Steele commands the trading floor with effortless confidence. As the city's top trader, she consistently surprises her peers with sharp intellect and an unmatched ability to generate profits. Her charm and playful flirting keep everyone captivated, while her analytical mind, shaped by a background in mathematics, finance, and NASA collaborations, gives her a unique edge. Vivian's cool, composed demeanor hides a fiercely competitive nature, and her strategic thinking ensures she stays ahead of the game. Always poised in her sharp business attire, she is a force to be reckoned with in the high-stakes world of finance.

Maxwell Dither is the epitome of chronic indecision in the trading world. Maxwell's talent lies not in making successful trades, but in annoying those around him with inventive excuses, envy, and excessive politeness. Despite spending all his time at the brokerage, rumors suggest he's never executed a single transaction. Maxwell is a living paradox—a character entrenched in the world of trading yet seemingly unable to commit to any action. His affliction with severe risk aversion only compounds his struggles, rendering him paralyzed by fear whenever an opportunity arises.

Victor Fortune is an eccentric risk-taker in the stock market. He relies on superstitions and gut feelings to inform his trades, interpreting signs from various sources such as traffic lights, license plates, or even subliminal messages in dice games. Despite his unorthodox approach, Victor consistently achieves profitable outcomes, baffling others with his seemingly innate ability. His unconventional methods and flashy appearance further contribute to the intrigue surrounding his enigmatic persona.

Meet **Mortimer Sagecroft**, a seasoned speculator known for his distinguished white hair and authoritative voice. Highly respected in his field, Mortimer is considered a veteran in speculation. However, despite his extensive knowledge, he struggles to mentor others due to his stern demeanor and the widespread ignorance among his trading colleagues. Mortimer doesn't say much, but when he does, it's with the weight of a lifetime of experience in financial markets. He's wary of newcomers looking for shortcuts. On the trading floor, Mortimer stands as a symbol of expertise, his wisdom shaped by years of market ups and downs.

Bradley Downfall is known for his incurable condition: chronic pessimism that influences every aspect of his trading. He firmly believes, without any doubt, that the markets will inevitably decline, regardless of any evidence suggesting otherwise. Additionally, he wakes up in a bad mood and goes to bed feeling even worse, constantly angry with everyone and everything, including the markets.

Meet **Carter Data**, a trader known for his love of numbers and data-driven decision-making. Carter meticulously analyzes market trends and financial data to uncover opportunities and risks. He believes in making informed decisions based on empirical evidence. However, despite his dedication to analysis, Carter sometimes faces unexpected challenges in the unpredictable world of financial markets. He learns that while numbers are powerful tools, they don't always guarantee success. This contrast between his methodical approach and the market's unpredictability shapes Carter's journey as a trader.

Meet **Ryder Riskmore**, a fearless trader who thrives on taking risks in the financial world. Ryder never hesitates to dive into investments, embracing uncertainty and the unknown. His motto is "nothing ventured, nothing gained," reflecting his belief that greater risks lead to greater rewards. Ryder's investment strategy involves high-stakes maneuvers, prioritizing potential gains over caution. He disregards cautionary tales and conservative approaches, preferring the excitement of navigating unpredictable market currents. While some may see Ryder's approach as reckless, he views it as a calculated dance with risk, often resulting in favorable outcomes. Ryder Riskmore proves that in finance, taking risks can lead to the most rewarding outcomes.

TRADING WITH THE GODS

Ryder Riskmore leaned back, his frustration evident. *"Gold is the most difficult asset to trade in the universe. Every time I trade gold futures, I end up losing... and always for different reasons!"*

Maxwell Dither nodded in agreement. *"Yes, gold is capricious... almost metamorphic. Sometimes it rises in a high-interest-rate environment, which is counterintuitive, or it devalues even when interest rates are falling. It's enough to drive a saint mad."*

Seizing the moment, Mortimer Sagecroft added, *"Maxwell, it's like you read my mind when you mentioned saints. Speculating on gold prices is almost divine. In many religious texts, gold is valuable and sacred. Being durable and resistant, it symbolizes immortality and eternity. Simply put..."*

Maxwell Dither interrupted smoothly, finishing Mortimer's thought, *"...the gods don't like humans speculating, directly or indirectly, on the price of gold. In many religious texts, gold is used as a metaphor for virtues and spiritual wealth..."*

"Exactly!" Mortimer agreed.

John Spinner cut in, exasperated. *"Geez, guys! You could have told me this sooner. Just last month, I blew my rent money on a trade in Majestic Gold (MGOD)."*

Mortimer chuckled. *"I don't think divine intervention played a role in your loss, John. It's just the same old story, unfortunately."*

Maxwell couldn't resist a joke. *"John, with a ticker like MGOD, all I can say is, 'My God!'"*

Ryder seized the opportunity to tease John further. *"Seems like if you keep losing rent money, you might have to ask Vivian for shelter. Maybe she'll let you sleep in the pantry if you make her breakfast every morning!"*

Everyone laughed at John's expense. At least he seemed to have found an external reason for his loss in Majestic Gold, even if the explanation was more celestial than terrestrial.

THE IPO

The atmosphere buzzed with excitement on the day of LunarLube's (LLUB) IPO. This cutting-edge space lubricant company had traders eager to jump in. John Spinner, ever the optimist, announced, *"I'm buying 400 shares at market price! Dinner tonight's on me, thanks to LunarLube!"* Ryder Riskmore, known for his bold risk-taking, also jumped in, purchasing 5,000 shares at market price and placing a limit order for another 5,000 at a discount.

In the midst of the frenzy, Maxwell Dither couldn't ignore Victor Fortune's unusual silence. Victor, who had been touting LLUB's potential for weeks, had yet to make a move. *"Victor,"* Maxwell probed, *"not feeling trigger-happy today? You were so bullish on LunarLube."*

Victor, unusually flustered, suddenly shouted, "Selling 10,000 shares of LunarLube at market! No, make it 15,000! Quick, quick! I'm shorting 15,000 shares, right?"

The room erupted in confusion. Shorting? The same Victor who had been predicting LunarLube's meteoric rise was now betting against it? John Spinner, astonished, yelled, *"Have you lost your mind, Victor? You're going to ruin yourself! Buy in with us while you can!"*

Victor, ignoring their frantic pleas, yelled back, *"Another 5,000 shorted! Hurry! I'll explain later... you wouldn't understand!"*

As the day unfolded, the wisdom—or perhaps the madness—of Victor's strategy became apparent. LunarLube's shares, buoyed by initial hype but lacking substance, nosedived. By the closing bell, LLUB had plummeted to its daily low, leaving a trail of dismayed investors.

Spinner, face buried in his hands, was already tallying his losses. Maxwell, despite having stayed out, looked like he'd aged a decade under the stress. Victor, meanwhile, reveled in the chaos, performing a victory dance that was more awkward than celebratory.

Maxwell, still stunned, finally asked, *"What made you switch your stance, Victor? Why did you bet against LunarLube?"*

Victor, grinning with a mix of confidence and mischief, replied, *"The stock was doomed from the start. Didn't you see? LLUB spells 'bull' backward! It had to be bearish, and bearish it was!"*

Maxwell could only stare in disbelief, muttering, *"Oh my God!"* The weight of Victor's seemingly nonsensical yet undeniably successful strategy hung heavily in the air.

Notes:

An IPO (Initial Public Offering) is the first sale of a company's shares to the public, allowing it to raise capital and become publicly traded on a stock exchange.

**Shorting a stock means betting that its price will fall;*

MORNING MIDAS

The atmosphere crackled with tension as Ryder Riskmore slammed his trading console shut and flung his shiny dark blue blazer onto a distant chair. "There I go again," he muttered, running a hand through his hair. "Start strong, only to fizzle out by the end of the trading session. Break-even, at best, and more often than not, a loss!"

Maxwell Dither, dressed in khaki trousers and a crisp white shirt, a man whose fingers seemed always ready to type a headline rather than place a trade order, chimed in, "Classic case of the midday slump, Ryder. You need some supplements. Boost those energy levels!"

John Spinner, eager to help, chimed in, "Tell you what, Ryder. My buddy at the corner market, he's from Senegal, swears by this stuff called Moringa. His mom makes these killer recipes, energy cocktails that'd raise the dead!"

Vivian Steele, the team's resident walking encyclopedia, delicately adjusted her exquisite and refined gemstone necklace before speaking with a faint smile. "Actually, John, the scientific name is Moringa oleifera. Originally from India, but cultivated in parts of Africa as well. It's renowned for its rich blend of vitamins, minerals, and antioxidants – reputedly excellent for boosting energy levels."

John flushed a charming shade of crimson, unable to handle even the slightest praise from Miss Steele without turning into a flustered mess.

Ryder, ever the joker, took a jab at Vivian's impressive memory. *"Miss Steele, that computer brain of yours must process more than just market data, huh? You must read a ton. And remember it all too. Unlike some of us who forget everything after a few days."*

Mortimer, the team's elder statesman, had been quietly observing the banter, his tolerance for idle chatter wearing thin with age. *"Ryder,"* he interjected, his voice gravelly but firm, *"The solution to your problem is far simpler than you think, and it doesn't involve any exotic African plants."*

Ryder, ever the skeptic, scoffed. *"Oh yeah? Enlighten me then, Mortimer. What's your miracle cure? Don't tell me you have a secret stash of anti-inflammatory joint juice that doubles as a trading superpower?"* A booming laugh erupted from him, clearly amused by his own joke.

Mortimer, with a stoicism honed by years in the market, countered, *"Forget magic potions, Ryder. Just trade in the morning. Then, for the afternoon? Take a walk, unwind with a book, hit the gym - whatever recharges you. Give your mind a break."*

Ryder's face fell. *"What? And miss out on all the action, the volatility of the closing hour? No way!"*

Mortimer shook his head, a touch of exasperation in his eyes. *"Worse than the blind man, Ryder,"* he sighed, *"is the one who refuses to see."* He crossed himself, a silent plea for Ryder to finally open his eyes to the obvious solution.

THE IMPOSSIBLE STREAK

Another tense day in the trading room, with John sweating bullets as he watches the stock he's shorting skyrocket...

John Spinner nervously taps his shoe on the base of his chair in a rhythmic pattern, *"I'm short on CyberFlare (CYBR) and the stock just keeps climbing! This is the fourth consecutive session it's been surging... it doesn't even pause to catch its breath! My account is getting decimated!"*

Carter Data, the junior analyst on duty, opens his research software and meticulously searches through CyberFlare's historical price data for the longest streaks of gains and losses. *"Four consecutive days of rising, you say? Let me check on ChartMaster Pro."* Adjusting his glasses, Carter looks at John seriously, *"John, a four-day rising streak isn't that rare. In my sample, the longest consecutive rise for this stock is nine days! And it wasn't that long ago... it was at the beginning of this year during the tech rally."*

Maxwell Dither, ever calm as he has no open positions and is merely a spectator, chimes in. *"The market is strong, and the tech sector is the most sought after by institutional investors right now. You've got a very risky position, John. It could rise for eight, ten consecutive days if the market stays this way. Protect yourself, John!*

It's better to close out before the damage gets worse. The first loss is the best loss."

John Spinner can barely hear anything, he's flushed and sweating, taking off his blazer and loosening his shirt, revealing his signature necklace. Every tick the stock rises seems to take a day off the poor guy's life.

Carter Data, listening to Maxwell's dispassionate comment, counters, *"Ten consecutive days, Maxwell? That's almost impossible, it's never happened!"*

Mortimer Sagecroft, who had been following the conversation with interest, adds wisely, *"Carter, old-timers like me who've been in this game for decades know well that in the stock market, the impossible happens about twice a year."*

John Spinner looks at Mortimer and swallows hard. He knows he's in trouble and that his pains are likely to get even worse...

Notes:

* *Shorting a stock means betting that its price will fall;*

** A tick in stock trading refers to the smallest possible price movement of a stock's price either up or down. It represents the minimum fluctuation in price that can occur during trading;

DOUBLE TROUBLE

John Spinner arrived at the office, ready to conquer the day, but his enthusiasm quickly turned to panic when he glimpsed the stock quotes.

"What's the deal with the tech stocks?" he exclaimed, turning to Maxwell Dither for answers.

"They're plummeting," Maxwell replied, his voice heavy with concern. "Michael Turner's aggressive sell recommendation this morning sent them into a tailspin."

John's eyes widened in disbelief. "But yesterday, I heard on the radio that Turner was super bullish on stocks in his sector! I rushed over here and bought up everything I could. How could his outlook change so drastically overnight?"

Maxwell shook his head. "Turns out, you heard about Matthew Turner, not Michael. Matthew is the Energy Stocks analyst, and they're twin brothers. It's a total mix-up."

John's frustration boiled over. "Twin brothers? I'm losing money because of a mix-up between twin brothers' names? This is unbelievable!"

Bradley Downfall chimed in, adding clarity to the chaos. *"Indeed, it was Matthew who was bullish on his sector yesterday. Michael's research came out this morning."*

Mortimer Sagecroft, always the voice of reason, offered a sobering assessment. *"This is what happens when you invest based on soundbites, John. You didn't even bother to verify the information. The market doesn't reward laziness or half-informed decisions."*

John's frustration turned to defensiveness. *"Seriously, Mortimer? You're going to hassle me too? Just take a break and go chill at home!"*

In a huff, John stormed out of the office, convinced that the universe was conspiring against him.

THE QUEEN OF QUANT

In the heart of the financial district, Carter Data was deeply engrossed in his world of stock market charts and graphs. His thick-rimmed glasses sat precariously on his nose as he leaned in, fingers tapping away at the keyboard with precision. With keen eyes scanning the data, he hunted for trading patterns and promising setups. Suddenly, a particular stock, Nexus Dynamics (NXDY), seized his attention.

Carter, intrigued by the potential of NXDY, turned to his colleague, Vivian Steele, a woman known for her sharp financial acumen. *"Miss Steele,"* he inquired, *"what do you think of Nexus Dynamics?"*

Vivian twirled her serpent-shaped ring as if focusing, then without hesitation, launched into a detailed analysis of the company, her voice filled with confidence and expertise. *"It operates within the software sector, boasting a market capitalization of $2 billion. Trading has fluctuated between $22 and $45 over the past year, hitting a peak three weeks ago and a low point in January. Recent sessions indicate an upward trend with moderate fluctuations."*

John Spinner, another colleague within earshot, was astonished by Vivian's rapid-fire recitation of financial data. *"What?"*

he exclaimed, his voice laced with disbelief, his flashy and embroidered shirt slightly rumpled as he leaned closer to hear better.

Carter, impressed by Vivian's knowledge, couldn't help but compliment her, *"Vivian, you sound like a computer!"*

Vivian, dressed in a sleek navy-blue power suit that accentuated her confident demeanor, greeted them with a warm smile. *"You can call me 'Vi' if you prefer,"* she said, her voice calm yet authoritative. Laughter rippled through the room at her casual suggestion, breaking the tension and easing John's nerves momentarily.

Bradley Downfall, renowned for his pessimistic market outlook, listened intently before interjecting, *"And what about the risks associated with the stock, Vivian? What's the bearish perspective?"*

Vivian delicately closed her fountain pen, until it was tightly closed, before calmly addressing Bradley's concerns, *"In this particular sector, there is intense competition, which exerts significant pressure on profit margins. Additionally, the recent appointment of a new CEO, who has a track record of instability, adds further complexity."*

Carter, thoroughly impressed by Vivian's comprehensive analysis, exclaimed, *"This is better than any Bloomberg terminal!"*

John, feeling a pang of inadequacy, confessed, *"I should've stayed in school and hit the books harder. I just feel so small compared to all this brainpower around me."*

Ryder Riskmore, injected a touch of humor into the conversation, *"John, your problem started way back with a lack of breast milk...but at least you turned out handsome!"*

The office erupted in laughter, while John's cheeks flushed with a hint of embarrassment. Despite his self-deprecating remarks, he couldn't help but be drawn to Vivian's intelligence and confidence, secretly admiring her from afar.

THE SIGNAL THAT MISLED CARTER

Carter Data sat nervously at his trading desk, his eyes glued to the monitors displaying charts and indicators. *"The buy and sell signals for GigaSoft Robotics (GIBO) using the VRS Oscillator have been disastrous,"* he muttered in frustration. *"I'm bleeding money... it told me to short sell when the stock was at $32, and now it's at $37!"*

Mortimer Sagecroft was absorbed in his morning routine, reading the Wall Street Times at his desk. Without looking up, he advised the young analyst nearby, *"Carter, if an indicator tells you what to do, something is seriously wrong."* He calmly kept reading the newspaper, projecting an air of composed authority.

Meanwhile, Vivian seizes the moment to bring up the GigaSoft Robotics (GIBO) chart on her trading workstation, adding the VRS Oscillator to assess the situation Carter Data finds himself in. *"Carter, the VRS Oscillator isn't well-suited for stocks with momentum like GIBO. It's designed for selling resistance and buying support in assets lacking strong momentum or abrupt short-term trends."*

Carter, beads of perspiration forming on his brow, leans forward slightly, his attention fully focused on Vivian's explanation. He asks with genuine curiosity, *"Miss Steele, do you typically incorporate the VRS Oscillator into your trading strategies?"*

Vivian leans back in her chair, crossing her legs slowly to reveal knee-high boots that accentuate her poised demeanor. With a graceful sweep, she runs a hand through her hair, exuding confidence as she responds with assuredness. Her every movement seems calculated yet effortlessly confident, commanding attention from those around her. *"Not as often these days, but I'm intimately familiar with the indicator—I developed it during my tenure at TradeMaster Pro..."*

John Spinner, in the midst of pouring his energy drink into a paper cup, suddenly seems electrified with excitement. He jumps in his chair, swiftly turning to face Miss Steele. *"You created the VRS? That's incredible, Vivian!"*

Carter Data, still trying to make sense of everything, asks, *"Miss Steele, what does VRS stand for?"*

"My dear Carter," Miss Steele says, her Plume d'Or fountain pen delicately placed on the desk, *"It stands for Vivian Rinaldi Steele."* Her voice carries a poised and confident cadence, infused with a subtle hint of intrigue. As she touches up her light red lipstick, her actions are precise and graceful, capturing the attention of her colleagues who hang on her every word. Vivian's mastery of subtle pauses adds to the allure of her presence, weaving a spell that mesmerizes those around her.

John Spinner can't believe what he just heard, *"Rinaldi?"* he exclaims visibly surprised.

"Yes, John. My mother is Italian, from Milano."

John whistles and exclaims, *"Mamma Mia!"*

John and Carter now begin to discern the multifaceted layers of Miss Steele's personality. Rooted in her Latin heritage, she exudes a unique blend of elegance, sophistication, and a subtle allure that captivates those around her. Her demeanor, marked by a graceful confidence and an occasional playful undertone, reflects a cultural richness that enhances her interactions. It's this combination of poise, subtlety, and a natural charm that renders her truly irresistible, leaving an indelible impression on anyone fortunate enough to engage with her.

Notes:

* Buy and sell signals in trading are indicators or triggers based on technical analysis that suggest optimal times to enter (buy) or exit (sell) positions in financial markets;

** A technical indicator is a mathematical calculation based on historical price, volume, or open interest data, used to forecast future market movements or identify trends and patterns in financial markets;

*** Short selling is the practice of selling borrowed securities with the expectation of buying them back at a lower price to profit from a decline in their value;

**** In technical analysis, "resistance" is a price level where upward movement is typically stopped, acting like a ceiling. "Support" is a price level where downward movement is typically stopped, acting like a floor. Traders use these levels to make decisions, as they can signal shifts in market trends.

***** Momentum in stock trading refers to the speed and strength of price movements in a particular direction, indicating the strength of buying or selling pressure;

A SEISMIC TRADE

The day was progressing calmly on Wall Street when suddenly the ticker flashed, *"Major Earthquake in Northern China: Qinghai with Damaged Infrastructure."* Vivian Steele leapt like an Olympic gymnast and fired off an order on the keyboard with lightning speed.

Maxwell Dither, in his usual eloquence, commented, *"That area is very prone to seismic activity; it's where India collides with the rest of Asia."* John Spinner didn't hear Maxwell's geology lesson, his eyes glued to Viviane.

"Carter, did you notice that as soon as the headline appeared on the monitors, Vi immediately placed an order? What did she do? Ask her!" John urged.

"There you go, John! So outgoing about almost everything and so shy with Miss Steele! Why, I wonder..." Carter replied.

"Come on! She definitely did something smart, but what?" John persisted.

Maxwell Dither looked at the quotes and exclaimed in surprise, "ArcadiaX Gaming (DIAX) is down 27%! Strange...could it be a glitch?"

Vivian quickly explained, "ArcadiaX produces 90% of its consoles around Qinghai. With the destruction that an earthquake like this causes to factories and road infrastructure, they won't have consoles available in stores for Christmas. Production was already slightly delayed and now the holiday season is irretrievably lost."

"Miss Steele, how do you know that ArcadiaX Gaming produces 90% of its consoles in Qinghai?!" Carter asked, amazed.

"I read it in the annual report. All the information is there."

"And the order you placed was related to that?" Carter continued.

"Yes, I was quick...one of the first to react or maybe the first. I managed to short sell 50,000 shares before the sell-off. I've got a good open profit on this position, capturing almost the entire sell-off. My week is made," Vivian responded confidently.

John whispered, "The week? I wish that were my entire year..."

Mortimer Sagecroft, who had listened with interest to the entire interaction, commented, "Well, I admire Maxwell's knowledge and broad cultural understanding. He knew Qinghai is in China's seismic zone and the geological reason for it. However, from a trading standpoint, that information had no value... Miss Steele, on the other hand, applied knowledge she had gathered and used it immediately upon seeing the headline. Preparation and knowledge truly pay off." As Joe Paterno wisely put it, "The will to win is important, but the will to prepare is vital.'"

John, visibly excited by Viviane's performance, threw at Maxwell, *"Hey, Dither! Looks like you've been reading the wrong books!"* Carter and John laughed, leaving Maxwell embarrassed.

Maxwell quickly slipped into his British fabric blazer and retorted, *"Your ignorance must be worth a fortune!"* He stepped outside for some fresh air, certain that his big trade was just waiting for the right mix of technicals, fundamentals, and his own risk tolerance. Maxwell had faith, even if he stood alone in it.

THE WATER BOTTLE MYSTERY

Amidst the frantic pace of the trading room, John Spinner seizes a moment to step away and refill his plastic cup at the water cooler. His fascination with Vivian leads his gaze to an unfamiliar glass water bottle resting on her trading desk. Intrigued, he turns to Carter and asks, *"Hey, Carter, have you noticed that weird water bottle on Vivian's desk?"*

Carter, deeply focused on managing multiple trades, grumbles with a serious tone, *"Come on, John. I'm trying to stay on top of my positions here. Why are we discussing the type of water Miss Steele drinks?"* His tone conveys a sense of urgency and concentration on his trading tasks.

John steps away momentarily but remains determined. He circles back to Vivian's desk with a singular focus, driven by his insatiable curiosity about the enigmatic Miss Steele, extending even to the choice of water she prefers.

"Vivian, are you busy?" John asks timidly. *"No, John. I'm stepping away for a moment. I'm off to grab a coffee downstairs. The coffee machine here is simply dreadful. How can I assist you?"* John, a bit flustered, replies, *"Nothing much. I just noticed that water bottle on

your desk and got curious. Never seen that brand in the supermarket before..."

Vivian smiles softly, a glint of intrigue in her eyes, as she leisurely slides off her tailored jacket. Beneath, her arms are slender and graceful, adorned with a meticulously crafted gold bracelet that shimmers with a mosaic of precious stones. With a deliberate touch, she picks up the bottle, her fingers curling around its smooth glass surface, her gesture akin to the finesse of handling a delicate artifact, revealing a glimpse of her refined taste and subtle elegance. *"Valle Nevado Alpine Water? I import it from high-altitude springs in the Andes Mountains. This exceptionally pure, oxygen-rich water has a fresh, invigorating taste. Its high oxygen content boosts my energy and mental clarity, while the unique minerals enhance hydration. It's a luxurious indulgence that keeps me at my best throughout the trading day."*

John stood there, momentarily stunned by Vivian's elegant explanation of her water choice. *"Nice pick, Vi. Nice pick."* he finally managed to say, his mind buzzing with questions. Every encounter with Vivian seemed to reveal a new facet of her sophistication. How much did she pay for that water? How had she discovered it? What other secrets did she hold, and how had she cultivated such exquisite tastes? Determined to uncover more, John hurried back to his desk, eager to share his latest discovery with Carter.

SLIM PROFITS

SlimGenix (SGNX) stocks are on the rise once again, and Ryder Riskmore had caught the upswing.

"Look at SlimGenix (SGNX) stocks," exclaimed Maxwell Dither. "They're climbing again!"

"They've surged 123% year to date!" Carter Data exclaimed, adjusting his glasses with a scholarly air. "I'm not entirely convinced if it's just a passing trend or if they've genuinely developed a game-changing product. We'll need to see if the company's underlying fundamentals can substantiate this stock appreciation over time..."

Bradley Downfall interjected cynically, "This is nothing but a fleeting frenzy! It'll enjoy a brief stint as a darling of Wall Street, only to inevitably disappoint with lackluster earnings and projections, crashing hard thereafter. It's a tired cycle that repeats itself endlessly in this market. It baffles me how traders still fall for these dubious promoters."

Meanwhile, Carter continued, undeterred by Bradley's pessimism. "Ryder has been long since the low $20s. It's at $42... or rather, $43 now. It just keeps going up!"

Maxwell chuckled, "The stock itself is gaining weight! What's Ryder's *reasoning for being so optimistic about the stocks?"*

Carter explained, *"He says he's done his research—talking to a few gym buddies who are trying to lose weight. He's convinced that SlimGenix (SGNX) pills are very effective, paired with highly appealing marketing. And because he believes in it, he's holding onto his position..."*

John Spinner chimed in skeptically, *"Sounds too simple..."*

Carter smirked, adding another layer to Ryder's conviction. *"Oh, and besides that, Ryder mentioned the other day he peeked into Miss Steele's trash can and saw a box of SlimTech pills. Given her striking appearance and nutritional knowledge, he's even more convinced of the stock's potential and doubled down on his position."*

Bradley, ever the voice of caution, warned, *"Don't get caught up in the hype, Spinner. It's just a passing trend, a hype that will cost those half-baked speculators dearly... the stocks will reverse and plummet to levels that smell like insolvency!"*

John chuckled at Bradley's unwavering skepticism. *"You never hold back, do you?"*

Carter smiled, shaking his head affectionately. *"That's just Bradley being... Bradley!"*

The group shared a laugh, enjoying the banter and camaraderie even as they debated the future of SlimGenix (SGNX) stocks in the volatile world of Wall Street.

Notes:

* Being "long" in a stock means you own it and expect its price to rise;

FROM DATES TO DEALS

The sluggish summer afternoon was punctuated only by the slow tick of the market and infrequent updates. That all changed in an instant when a breaking news flash lit up the ticker and the financial channels throughout the room: *"Breaking News: ViewStream Set to Acquire BingeBox at 35% Premium!"*

The tranquility shattered as traders scrambled to understand the implications of this announcement. However, Victor Fortune and Vivian Steele remained unnervingly calm, a smugness that grated on their colleagues. Carter, trying to fully grasp the news, noticed Victor sitting idly with a satisfied expression. He asked, *"Victor, aren't you reacting to this? Aren't you going to open any positions?"*

Victor grabbed his calculator, glanced at the monitor, quickly did the math, and replied, *"I'm already up $25,000. Why bother?"*

Victor's arrogance was starting to annoy his colleagues, prompting Maxwell to dig deeper. *"Victor, did you already own shares of BingeBox?"*

Leaning back in his chair and sipping his energy drink, Victor replied, *"You won't believe what happened the other day. I set up a date on FlirtZone, and the girl was a bit nervous, so we agreed to meet at The Classic Ember. She was late, and while I was waiting, two* executives at the next table were discussing movies and series. Since I'm always looking for new things to watch, I leaned in a bit to listen. I quickly realized one was the CEO of ViewStream and the other the new CEO of BingeBox. They finished their dinner, shook hands, and said, 'Together we are stronger!'"

Maxwell exclaimed, "What? What are the odds of something like that happening?"

Victor shrugged. "Probably zero for you, but I doubt you'd have the guts to act on that information. How many things could go wrong? Right, Maxwell?"

The other colleagues laughed, though they were still perplexed by what they had heard. Meanwhile, Carter remembered, *"How did you know ViewStream was going to buy BingeBox at a premium?"*

With a confident demeanor, Victor rolled up the sleeves of his white shirt, loosened his colorful tie, and said, *"It seemed likely that a larger company would acquire a smaller one. To avoid any issues, I asked Vivian what deals would make sense in this sector..."*

Vivian, overhearing the conversation, approached in her black stiletto heels, black skirt, and chic pearl-colored blouse, exuding both professionalism and allure. *"Yes, Victor asked me what would make sense for streaming companies in terms of mergers and acquisitions. I had been studying the sector for some time, and considering the catalogs of films and series from various companies, as well as their subscriber numbers and capital positions, the smart move would be for ViewStream to acquire BingeBox."*

"*You told Vivian, not us?*" Carter questioned.

Victor quickly countered, "*No, Carter, I didn't tell anyone. I was worried the news would spread and be seen as insider trading, or that the CEOs would back out of the deal if there was a suspicion of a leak coming from them...*"

Vivian added, "*When Victor asked me, I had already acquired a significant position in BingeBox. That deal was the only one that made sense, so I decided to get ahead of it.*"

Mortimer processed all the information and concluded, "*Excellent. Victor is the perfect mix of luck and street smarts. He acts on the information he has, without fear, while Vivian reached the same conclusion without overhearing the conversation, but by doing the math and considering all the strategic options available in the sector. I'm too old for this kind of business, but I'm very happy to see talent in the office.*"

Maxwell, feeling a bit pinched and always considering himself the smartest in the office, shot back, "*Mortimer, I never thought you'd confuse luck with talent!*" He made a quick exit before anyone could engage him in a conversation that was becoming increasingly uncomfortable. As if it wasn't enough that Victor and Vivian were making money, now Mortimer had to praise them too?

Notes:

* *A premium on a buyout is the amount by which the purchase price of* *a company exceeds its current market value;*

** Insider trading is the illegal buying or selling of a company's stock based on non-public, material information about the company;

THE BAGEL SHOP TRADE

On the day of Aquagen Solutions (AQUA)'s earnings announcement, everyone stayed late for the after-hours session to witness the real-time release of results. Seemingly, no one held positions in the stock, but in reality, that wasn't entirely true.

As the countdown to the announcement began, anticipation filled the room. John Spinner, always optimistic, grinned and exclaimed, *"Let the fireworks begin! It's going to be like the closing show at DisneyWorld!"* His excitement was palpable.

Maxwell Dither, the eternal skeptic, shook his head. *"This type of stock attracts nothing but gamblers, gunslingers. Earnings for this are like playing the lottery. I'd never touch a stock like this,"* he asserted confidently. Under his breath, John muttered, *"Not in any way..."*

Maxwell continued, his tone a mix of disbelief and disdain. *"Aquagen Solutions (AQUA) shares just surged 40% last week, it's insane!"*

Carter Data, the group's junior analyst, contributed some numbers to the discussion. *"I've got the expected volatility for these earnings. Options are pricing in a 30% move up or down with the earnings release,"* he said, displaying detailed charts on his screen.

Mortimer Sagecroft, the voice of experience, cautioned, *"Those on the wrong side will learn a hard lesson. If they're heavily leveraged, they might blow up their trading accounts."* His words hung heavily in the air, a stark reminder of the risks involved.

"Where's Miss Steele when we need her most?" John Spinner asked. *"If she were here, I'd ask for her take on AQUA's prospects... Maybe hitch a ride on her insights, things have been tough lately..."*

Carter Data replied, *"You know she rarely trades on Wednesday afternoons. She's usually doing pro bono work for a nature conservation foundation."*

Suddenly, the room buzzed with activity as the results flashed across the ticker. Earnings printed just slightly below consensus, and the stock unexpectedly plummeted 35% in an instant. The reaction was swift and intense.

Ryder Riskmore celebrated as if his team had scored a goal, leaving everyone staring at him in confusion. Maxwell, always quick to question, asked, *"What's going on, Ryder? Are you having a seizure?"*

With a triumphant smile, Ryder responded, *"I'm cashing in big time! I had a massive short position* on AQUA, and with this drop, I'm making a killing!"* His excitement was contagious, though it left some feeling a bit envious.

John Spinner looked at him, surprised. *"And you didn't tell anyone? I could have jumped in! I could really use a win..."*

Maxwell, never one to miss an opportunity for his classic skepticism, inquired, "What was your rationale? Were you just playing the lottery?"

Ryder, enjoying the spotlight, began to explain. "Jose, the Colombian guy at the café across the street, told me this morning he was hyped about Aquagen's stock. He knew it was going to move big today, but didn't know why exactly."

Raising an eyebrow, Maxwell asked, "Jose from the Coffee & Bagel shop?"

"Yeah!" Ryder continued. "He mentioned all his buddies had been buying the stock in recent weeks. It was all the talk in his neighborhood. So, Carter had shown me a study suggesting crowded trades often burst, so I took a shot."

Impressed, Carter nodded. "Risk-taking, but well played! Theory meets practice, nicely done."

Ryder had turned street smarts into a memorable trade, transforming an ordinary day into an extraordinary one.

Notes:

* A short position is when an investor sells a borrowed asset, expecting its price to drop, so they can buy it back later at a lower price for a profit.

A MISUNDERSTANDING OF FELINE PROPORTIONS

Vivian, drained from a brutal trading session, kicked off her stiletto and massaged her aching foot. *"Guys,"* she sighed, *"I'm toast. Canceling my massage - I just need to crash on the couch with my love."*

John Spinner swivelled in his chair, ears perked like a startled puppy. *"Love?"* he blurted, his gaze darting to Carter Data. *"Did Vivian snag a boyfriend? You know anything, Carter?"*

Carter, perpetually detached from office gossip, shrugged. *"Relax, John. Pretty sure it's her cat. Heard her on the phone with the vet, calling it 'my love'..."*

John, still curious, leaned towards Vivian. *"Hey Viv, do you have a cat? What's its name?"*

Vivian smiled, a genuine warmth radiating from her. *"Of course, John! He's my whole world - couldn't imagine life without him. A Russian Blue, his name's Gorba."*

Mortimer, strolling by, stopped in his tracks. *"Gorba, eh? Now that's a perfect name!"*

John, completely lost, frowned. *"Gorda? Isn't that Spanish for... fat?"* He chuckled awkwardly. *"My downstairs neighbors are Dominican, and the husband always calls his wife 'mi gorda' playfully."*

A wave of laughter washed over the office. John's cluelessness was a constant source of amusement. Oblivious, he puffed out his chest, proud of his Spanish knowledge.

Mortimer, ever the patient one, offered a gentle correction. *"Gorba, John. Like Mikhail Gorbachev, the last leader of the Soviet Union."*

John's face fell. *"Ah, Gorba! History... never was my strong suit."* He mumbled, earning a final jab from Carter.

Carter, wiping his glasses with a flourish, couldn't resist a parting shot. *"And never will be, John. Never will be..."*

JUICY TRADE

John Spinner had read a headline on the front page of The Financial Tribune a few weeks ago, predicting that the orange harvest in Florida would be affected by adverse weather and that prices could skyrocket by summer. With the help of his broker, he set up a speculative position in Florida Orange futures, hoping this meteorological disaster would cause orange prices to soar, resulting in a rare profitable deal.

Upon arriving at the trading room, he receives a notification about the approaching expiration of his futures contract and the need to close his position. He closely watches the quotes, anxiously looking for the price of Florida Orange futures.

"75 bid / 102 ask? Are you kidding me? What kind of spread is this? I can only sell at 75? There's zero liquidity here! How is the spread this wide?"

Carter Data, calmly at his desk, asks, *"At what price did you enter?"*

John replies, *"I got in at 100. I wanted to sell at 101-102, but not a single trade has gone through for hours… and now I got a notice to close the contract today or I'll have to go to delivery? What delivery? Sounds like I'm running a food truck!"*

Maxwell: *"Yes, indeed, the Florida Orange futures show no bids at all. The market depth looks more like Gukanjima Island*."*

John Spinner: *"Stop with the stories, Dither! I have a serious problem on my hands. How am I going to get out of this position without taking a huge loss?"*

Mortimer Sagecroft, passing by on his slow walk to his mid-morning tea, stops next to John. *"It's the problem with trading assets with little or no liquidity, John. Plus, it's a futures contract you let get too close to the first notice date. Now, liquidity is minimal, and the spreads are wide."*

John Spinner: *"First notice? Damn, Mortimer. It sounds like a court notice; it scares me."*

Mortimer, with the patience of Job, reassures John by explaining the terminology used in the futures market. *"The first notice on a futures contract is when the seller of the contract must notify the buyer of their intention to deliver the underlying asset. Or, in this case, you would have to physically pick up the oranges corresponding to the contract you purchased."*

John, stunned and frightened, asks, *"Picking up the oranges? How... by truck? Where from?"*

Viviane Steele approached John, exuding the essence of spring in her outfit. Her attire featured floral patterns, complemented by 7 cm high-heeled sandals that accentuated her elegant stride. A hint of citrus-scented perfume lingered around her, adding to her allure as she addressed John.

"If you let the first notice slip by," she began, her voice smooth yet tinged with concern, *"you'll find yourself having to collect a ton of oranges from a warehouse in the Greater Miami Area. Doesn't sound like a smart move, does it, John?"*

Ryder, more amused than ever with the mess Spinner has gotten into, quips, *"Don't worry, we can help you pick up the merchandise! I know a friend of the Mayor, and maybe we can convince him to organize something like the Tomatina**, but with oranges! What do you think? It would be fun!"*

Carter: *"Miami Beach would be a great spot for a quick getaway, John. Maybe you can talk Miss Steele into joining you. I can already see you there, the Orange King or just O.K., with a real queen by your side!"*

John Spinner: *"O.K.? I'm totally K.O.!!!"*

Notes:

* Gukanjima Island, off Nagasaki's coast, was a thriving coal mining site during Japan's industrialization but has been abandoned since the 1970s. Its densely packed concrete buildings create a stark, eerie atmosphere, likened to a ghost town rising from the sea;

** The Tomatina is a renowned festival in Buñol, Spain, where people throw tomatoes at each other in a lively and colorful event held annually in August;

SURFING THE MARKETS

In a high-rise trading room in downtown Manhattan, the atmosphere was electric with the focused energy of the traders.

Ryder Riskmore closely monitored the charts, waiting for the perfect moment to strike. He opened a trade on Nasdaq futures, held the position for a few minutes, then closed it and reclined in his chair, sipping his blueberry energy drink.

Mortimer, always attuned to the pulse of the trading room, not only knew who was winning or losing for the day but also had a general sense of everyone's positions. *"Ryder, I've noticed you have an extraordinary knack for intraday trading with Nasdaq futures,"* he remarked.

Ryder, surprised that Mortimer had been observing his trades, responded with a playful tone, *"Mortimer, I picked up this technique back when I lived in California…"*

Maxwell Dither, who always felt uneasy about his colleagues' successes, questioned skeptically, *"Ryder, how did you manage to trade the Nasdaq from California with the time zone difference? Did you wake up at five in the morning to trade?"*

Ryder laughed. *"Don't be ridiculous, Maxwell! I wasn't trading when I lived in California. I was living in Bolsa Chica with my girlfriend at the time, near Huntington Beach."

Vivian, leaning forward with curiosity and a hint of admiration in her eyes, urged Ryder, *"Ryder, you've got to tell us more! That sounds like such an adventure—what was it really like living and working in Bolsa Chica?"*

"Well," Ryder continued, *"I surfed all day, every day. I gave surf lessons and worked at a nearby bar in the evenings. When I started trading here in New York, I realized that surfing and intraday trading Nasdaq futures have a lot in common..."*

Maxwell, visibly irritated by what he considered a trivial comparison for someone who studied the markets as diligently as he did, snapped, *"You must have taken in a lot of saltwater out there..."*

Ryder, enjoying the chance to tease Maxwell, was delighted. *"Relax, Maxwell. Let me explain. In surfing, you anticipate the wave's direction and position your board accordingly. When the wave approaches, you adjust, paddle, and let it carry you, harnessing its energy. Since there's no surfing in Manhattan, I ride the waves of the Nasdaq. I wait for the right moment and then I ride it."* He laughed confidently.

Vivian was captivated by Ryder's description. *"That's an excellent analogy. I've never heard such a vivid description of a trading strategy. So, it turns out the best intraday Nasdaq futures trading course is at Bolsa Chica... Who would've thought, right, Maxwell?"*

Everyone laughed at Maxwell, who was seething with envy over Ryder's success and the acclaim he received. Maxwell had been searching for the perfect market entry for months and felt frustrated by these casual traders, especially when they managed to be profitable.

THE THREE-WORD CHALLENGE

When the trading session slows down and the market doesn't demand full attention, traders often seize the opportunity to chat. Carter Data, the young analyst, sparks the conversation with a challenge. *"I've got a fun exercise for us. Each of us has to describe our trading in just three words…"*

Riskmore, ever energetic, adjusts in his chair, rolls up the sleeves of his striking midnight blue shirt, and confidently declares, *"Carter, I'm a COOL-BLOODED KILLER!"* Before John Spinner can even respond, Ryder adds, *"And John… A SUICIDE BOMBER! He's a danger to himself and everyone around him!"*

Laughter fills the room. Ryder clearly gets the spirit of the exercise and is enjoying it, which annoys Bradley Downfall. *"What nonsense, Carter! I don't participate in silly games!"*

Vivian, impeccably dressed in a crisp white blouse with an embroidered collar and dark tailored pants, pairs her look with black pumps and a gold watch. As she works at her well-organized desk—stacked with financial and research reports—she looks up and says, *"Come on, Bradley, don't be so uptight! We all need to unwind a little."*

Bradley storms out of the room, visibly frustrated, muttering to himself, *"As if the markets rising wasn't enough, now they want me to join these games!"*

Vivian, watching him go, says, *"Some people just can't lighten up… Anyway, back to the game. I'd describe my trading as… RESEARCH THEN TRADE. I know, boring as hell!"*

Ryder glances over at Maxwell, who is trying to blend into the background in one of the back seats, knowing he's next. *"And let's not forget the great Maxwell! Easy one: NO TRADE TODAY!"*

As everyone laughs, Maxwell pretends not to hear and continues reading his research notes, though he's clearly blushing. His headphones are on, but as always, they're silent. Maxwell thinks he's undercover, or at least he likes to believe so.

SPLIT SAGA

John hurried into the trading room, already late for the morning session. He quickly scanned his monitor, only to freeze in shock.

"Yo, what's up with Fusion NanoDevices (FUNA)?" John blurted out, his voice tinged with panic. "The stocks are tanking 90%! I've got nearly all my cash in FUNA. How's that even happening?!"

Carter, relaxed because he didn't hold any position in the stock, leaned over. "Hold on, John. It looks like they did a stock split."

"A stock-strip? What the heck?" John's confusion was obvious.

Ryder Riskmore seized the opportunity to tease, bursting into laughter. "Hey, Spinner, I already know where you were last night, you sly dog! No use pretending otherwise!"

John felt a twinge of embarrassment, realizing his slip might have revealed more than he intended.

"Chill out, Ryder!" John cut in quickly, cheeks turning a bit red. "Quit with the jokes. Miss Steele might hear and get the wrong idea. Keep it clean."

Ignoring the banter, Mortimer stepped forward, ready to clarify.

"John, a stock split means..."

John's mind, always on overdrive, cut off Mortimer. "Oh, I get it, now! Like a banana split! Speaking of which, I could really use one right now..."

Carter chuckled, shaking his head. "When it comes to sweets, John, you're the real expert!"

Mortimer resumed, his patience akin to a seasoned educator. "Listen, John. In a 10-1 stock split, like this one, shareholders receive ten shares for every one they held before. At the same time, the stock price adjusts downwards by a factor of ten. That's why it appears to have dropped 90%. But in reality, the total value of your investment remains unchanged."

The realization hit John. "So, instead of a hundred shares, I now have a thousand? Feels like I've leveled up as a trader."

Vivian approached with her black stilettos echoing on the floor with every confident step she took. "Studies indicate that in the short term, stock splits often appeal to small investors who prefer holding a greater number of shares, even while the overall value remains unchanged."

Maxwell, always ready with a metaphor, chimed in. "It's like the placebo effect in the stock market."

Vivian nodded in agreement. "Exactly, Maxwell. Nicely articulated."

With the room now hushed, Vivian glided away, her stilettos punctuating the silence with each precise step. John felt a jolt as he fixated on the sharp clack of her heels against the polished wood floor, a reminder of her commanding presence in both the world of markets and his own swirling thoughts.

PIG PANIC

It was an unusual day on Wall Street when the swine industry became the hot topic. Typically immune to the fluctuations of agriculture, the financial district was now gripped by the news of a mysterious porcine virus threatening the swine sector. The virus, first detected on a small farm in Mexico, had quickly spread to Texas and then across the entire United States.

Carter Data, a junior chart analyst, observed, *"Sunny Acres Pork (SUNY) has been on a nine-day downward spiral. Things are looking grim."*

Maxwell, well-informed, nodded in agreement. *"No surprise there. A fatal pig virus, dubbed Porcine Fever, has emerged."*

John Spinner was visibly distressed. *"I don't get it! Finance World Network said the virus only spreads sexually between pigs. So I bought SUNY when it dipped, and now I'm in the red!"*

Vivian Steele, dressed in a sleek, tailored suit and stilettos that clicked decisively against the polished marble floor, rolled her eyes with an exasperated sigh. *"John, that's absurd,"* she said, her voice dripping with sarcasm. *"If the virus is sexually transmitted and difficult to detect, pigs can't reproduce. No piglets mean no pork, which means no product for Sunny Acres!"* She punctuated her statement with a sharp flick of her wrist, her silver bangles jangling.

Across the room, Maxwell, a conservative figure in both looks and manners, shifted slightly in his chair. His meticulously combed hair and perfectly pressed suit contrasted starkly with Vivian's bold presence. His eyes lit up, a rare spark of excitement breaking through his usually composed demeanor. *"That's what I call second-order thinking, Vivian. Impressive!"* he said, his voice measured but carrying an undertone of genuine admiration. He adjusted his tie, a subtle nod of approval accompanying his words, as he leaned forward ever so slightly, fully engaged in the conversation.

John groaned. "Where were you when I was about to buy this pig slop?"

Ryder Riskmore, ever the opportunist, chimed in, *"Cheer up, Spinner. That ham you got as a gift might be worth a fortune soon!"*

Everyone erupted in laughter, with Maxwell leading the charge. *"Absolutely, Ryder. Investment potential!"*

The trading floor was filled with the sound of laughter, proving that even in the face of turmoil, humor can prevail.

COPPER GLOW

As the trading session approached its final stretch on Wall Street, tension mounted when the screens abruptly flashed: *"Breaking News: Assassination Attempt on Esteban Rojas..."* Viviane Steele's eyes darted to the screens for a fleeting moment before her intense focus returned to her trading station. With swift precision, she unleashed a flurry of orders, each keystroke echoing the urgency of the unfolding situation.

Carter Data, who was nearby, queried sharply, *"Who in the world is Esteban Rojas?"*

John Spinner shot back, *"Sounds like a Mexican cartel beef or something."*

Observing Vivian's swift actions after the headline, Carter inquired with intensity, *"Miss Steele, who exactly is Esteban Rojas? And how does this headline affect the trading action?"*

Miss Steele, seated at her trading desk in a black pencil skirt and pristine white silk blouse, epitomized poise under pressure. Her perfectly defined eyebrows framed eyes that darted across multiple screens, while her sharply cut stiletto heels tapped rhythmically against the floor. With an emphatic wave of her hand and a silent *"Wait"* mouthed from her bold red lips, Viviane signaled her focus. She had already opened massive positions, strategically poised to capitalize on the market movements triggered by the headline.

Meanwhile, Maxwell had time to open the developing news story and added, *"Esteban Rojas is the charismatic leader of Chilean mine workers. He's a communist negotiating for higher wages and better working conditions. This could impact copper prices and companies that own copper mines."*

Carter persisted, *"Miss Steele? Enlighten us."*

Viviane paused for a moment, adjusting her skirt to ensure the lace of her stockings remained discreetly hidden. She then spoke with the calm authority of a seasoned Wall Street trader. *"This headline is likely to drive up copper prices and boost the stocks of copper mining companies in Peru and Australia. Esteban Rojas is a revered figure among Chilean copper miners, who will likely strike and halt production. Consequently, I immediately bought copper futures and shares of Outback Copper Corp. (OCC) and Peruvian Copper Resources (PCOP) as soon as the headline broke, managing to secure an early entry price. Speed of execution is critical in these situations. Now, with these initial profits, I can strategically manage the position moving forward."*

John Spinner asked, *"Why those choices, Viv?"*

"With copper production in Chile expected to take a significant hit, there will be less supply, which typically translates to higher commodity prices. Who stands to gain while Chilean mines are

offline?" Vivian replied thoughtfully, her hand deftly sketching a diagram in her notebook with a sleek fountain pen. The fine nib glided smoothly across the page, leaving a trail of deep indigo ink. Each stroke was precise and deliberate, reflecting her meticulous analysis of market dynamics.

John sported a boldly patterned shirt in shades of salmon and vibrant blue, paired with a chain around his neck and a mane of voluminous, curly hair. His flashy ensemble exuded a unique charm that catered to a specific taste.

"Yo, Viv, this is getting way over our heads," John remarked, gesturing to the complex topic at hand.

Vivian leans back gracefully, skillfully pinning up her hair. *"The Australian and Peruvian copper miners. After Chile, the world's largest copper producer, countries like Peru and Australia are next in line. Having meticulously analyzed the earnings reports of nearly every major copper company worldwide, I expect these two to benefit the most from the market's response."*

Mortimer Sagecroft interjected with a refined air, *"This is the intersection of preparation and opportunity, my dear. Those countless hours devoted to poring over research, annual reports, and commodity analyses yield dividends, not just in the future, but in the present moment. Splendid foresight, Miss Steele."*

John Spinner and Carter Data looked on in disbelief. Carter harbored aspirations of becoming a trader as astute as Vivian, realizing that beyond meticulously studying every traded asset and its interrelations, he needed to cultivate quick reflexes and unwavering composure to seize aggressive opportunities without delay. In the trading room, the adage *"time is money"* resonated more profoundly than anywhere else.

FROM VEGAS TO WALL STREET: THE VICTOR FORTUNE STORY

On a sweltering day in New York, Carter, John, and Maxwell decide to grab coffee at a quaint café in a nearby plaza. Maxwell is preoccupied with thoughts of Victor Fortune's extraordinary luck, feeling as though Victor possesses an invisible shield that wards off misfortune. To Maxwell, Victor seems almost otherworldly, as if he hails from another galaxy and is blessed with unparalleled fortune.

When Carter offers to get the coffees, Maxwell seizes the moment to ask John Spinner about Victor's background, eager to uncover more. *"John, where did Victor Fortune come from? What's his story? He doesn't seem like the typical Wall Street trader..."*

John takes a breath, adjusts his chain, rolls up the sleeves of his colorful shirt, and replies, *"Ah, that lucky guy. Victor Fortune hails from Las Vegas, his natural habitat. He cleaned out the casinos there for months, hitting jackpots on the slot machines."*

Maxwell, eyes wide, processes the information. *"That makes more sense now. Why did he leave Las Vegas? It seems like the perfect place for someone with his kind of luck."*

John explains, *"It's the usual tale. He cleaned out the Mirage Royal and was politely asked never to return. Then he moved to the Golden Mirage and continued hitting jackpots on the slots and 21s in blackjack... he attracted a lot of attention. One day, while in a supermarket parking lot on the Strip, three goons showed up and gave him a severe beating. They warned him never to come back to Las Vegas and said it was his final warning. He took the hint and left quietly."*

Maxwell is astonished. *"Wow, that's quite a story!"*

John adds, *"So he ended up on Wall Street, where he can win without getting threatened or beaten up. He even affectionately calls it Calle del Muro."*

Maxwell, looking stunned, replies, *"Calle del Muro? How dare he disrespect Manhattan like that!"*

Maxwell heads back to the office slowly, mulling over Victor's incredible story and realizing that nothing would please him more than seeing Victor face a streak of bad luck. But given how things are going, that seems pretty unlikely.

ABOUT THE AUTHOR

Henrique M. Simões

 Henrique M. Simões is a seasoned futures trader with over two decades of expertise in decoding the intricate world of short-term trading patterns. From the early stages of his career, Henrique was captivated by the dynamic nature of financial markets, leading him on a relentless pursuit of knowledge and mastery in the art of trading.

With a wealth of hands-on experience accumulated over 20-plus years, Henrique has honed his skills in navigating the complexities of the market, specializing in short-term trading strategies that require a keen understanding of market dynamics and swift decision-making. His unique insights into trading patterns have not only withstood the test of time but have consistently yielded success in the fast-paced world of futures trading.

BOOKS BY THIS AUTHOR

Trading Tales: Adventures In The Stock Market

This book is a collection of funny stories about traders who gather at a brokerage to conduct business in the stock market. Rivalries, conflicts, and envy take hold of the characters involved in picturesque episodes.

Inspired by actual individuals I've encountered throughout my career in trading, spanning both brokerage firms and hedge funds, these stories provide glimpses into the colorful characters that populate the trading world.

From seasoned veterans to ambitious newcomers, the brokerage is a melting pot of diverse personalities, each with their own unique approach to the market. Amidst the buzz of trading terminals and ringing phones, rivalries simmer, conflicts flare up, and envy rears its head, driving the narrative forward with palpable energy and tension.

Trading Tales: The Ticker Never Stops - Volume 2

This book is the second part of a series of humorous tales about traders congregating at a brokerage to navigate the complexities of the stock market. Within these stories, the characters find themselves entangled in rivalries, conflicts, and bouts of envy, painting vivid scenes of their experiences.

Vivian Steele: The Queen Of Wall Street

Step into the fast-paced world of finance with Vivian Steele, where sharp intellect meets stunning style. Revered as the city's foremost trader, Vivian's strategic brilliance and unparalleled ability to turn chaos into profit are matched only by her striking appearance and commanding presence. From her beginnings as a quantitative analyst to her current status as a trailblazer in trading, Vivian navigates the financial markets with a blend of mathematical precision and intuitive insight. As she glides through boardrooms and trading floors in killer stilettos, her cool demeanor and playful charm keep colleagues and competitors alike captivated. In "The Queen of Wall Street," witness Vivian Steele redefine success in the world of high finance, one meticulously calculated trade at a time.

www.ingramcontent.com/pod-product-compliance
Lightning Source LLC
Chambersburg PA
CBHW070408230526
45471CB00006B/2709